North American Folklore

Folk Speech

BY SHIRLEY BRINKERHOFF

Mason Crest Publishers

Mason Crest Publishers Inc.
370 Reed Road
Broomall, Pennsylvania 19008
(866) MCP-BOOK (toll free)
www.masoncrest.com

First printing
1 2 3 4 5 6 7 8 9 10
Library of Congress Cataloging-in-Publication Data on file at the Library of Congress.
ISBN 1-59084-345-2
      1-59084-328-2 (series)

Design by Lori Holland.
Composition by Bytheway Publishing Services, Binghamton, New York.
Cover design by Joe Gilmore.
Printed and bound in the Hashemite Kingdom of Jordan.

Picture credits:
Comstock: p. 98
Corel: pp. 22, 90
Corbis: pp. 6, 38, 40, 58, 60, 82
PhotoDisc: pp. 56, 80
J. Rowe: pp. 8, 12, 14, 17, 24, 26, 29, 30, 32, 33, 34, 35, 36, 37, 42, 47, 53, 54, 55, 67,
        70, 72, 74, 75 ,77, 78, 79, 84, 86, 89, 91
Cover: "Fourth of July Speech" by J. C. Leyendecker © 1908 SEPS: Licensed by Curtis
        Publishing, Indianapolis, IN. www.curtispublishing.com

Contents

Folklore grows from long-ago
seeds. Just as an acorn sends
down roots even as it shoots up
leaves across the sky, folklore is
rooted deeply in the past and
yet still lives and grows today.
It spreads through our modern
world with branches as wide
and sturdy as any oak's;
it grounds us in yesterday even
as it helps us make sense of
both the present and the future.

Introduction

by Dr. Alan Jabbour

WHAT DO A TALE, a joke, a fiddle tune, a quilt, a jig, a game of jacks, a saint's day procession, a snake fence, and a Halloween costume have in common? Not much, at first glance, but all these forms of human creativity are part of a zone of our cultural life and experience that we sometimes call "folklore."

The word "folklore" means the cultural traditions that are learned and passed along by ordinary people as part of the fabric of their lives and culture. Folklore may be passed along in verbal form, like the urban legend that we hear about from friends who assure us that it really happened to a friend of their cousin. Or it may be tunes or dance steps we pick up on the block, or ways of shaping things to use or admire out of materials readily available to us, like that quilt our aunt made. Often we acquire folklore without even fully realizing where or how we learned it.

Though we might imagine that the word "folklore" refers to cultural traditions from far away or long ago, we actually use and enjoy folklore as part of our own daily lives. It is often ordinary, yet we often remember and prize it because it seems somehow very special. Folklore is culture we share with others in our communities, and we build our identities through the sharing. Our first shared identity is family identity, and family folklore such as shared meals or prayers or songs helps us develop a sense of belonging. But as we grow older we learn to belong to other groups as well. Our identities may be ethnic, religious, occupational, or regional—or all of these, since no one has only one cultural identity. But in every case, the identity is anchored and strengthened by a variety of cultural traditions in which we participate and share with our neighbors. We feel the threads of connection with people we know, but the threads extend far beyond our own immediate communities. In a real sense, they connect us in one way or another to the world.

Folklore possesses features by which we distinguish ourselves from each other. A certain dance step may be African American, or a certain story urban, or a certain hymn Protestant, or a certain food preparation Cajun. Folklore can distinguish us, but at the same time it is one of the best ways we introduce ourselves to each other. We learn about new ethnic groups on the North American landscape by sampling their cuisine, and we enthusiastically adopt musical ideas from other communities. Stories, songs, and visual designs move from group to group, enriching all people in the process. Folklore thus is both a sign of identity, experienced as a special marker of our special groups, and at the same time a cultural coin that is well spent by sharing with others beyond our group boundaries.

Folklore is usually learned informally. Somebody, somewhere, taught us that jump rope rhyme we know, but we may have trouble remembering just where we got it, and it probably wasn't in a book that was assigned as homework. Our world has a domain of formal knowledge, but folklore is a domain of knowledge and culture that is learned by sharing and imitation rather than formal instruction. We can study it formally—that's what we are doing now!—but its natural arena is in the informal, person-to-person fabric of our lives.

Not all culture is folklore. Classical music, art sculpture, or great novels are forms of high art that may contain folklore but are not themselves folklore. Popular music or art may be built on folklore themes and traditions, but it addresses a much wider and more diverse audience than folk music or folk art. But even in the world of popular and mass culture, folklore keeps popping up around the margins. E-mail is not folklore—but an e-mail smile is. And college football is not folklore—but the wave we do at the stadium is.

This series of volumes explores the many faces of folklore throughout the North American continent. By illuminating the many aspects of folklore in our lives, we hope to help readers of the series to appreciate more fully the richness of the cultural fabric they either possess already or can easily encounter as they interact with their North American neighbors.

Folk speech is the ordinary language, vocabulary, names, and jokes of ordinary people.

ONE

A Vocabulary
All Our Own

Identity and Speech

The syntax of folk English sometimes sounds amusing—as in the Pennsylvania German sentence: "Throw Mama from the train a kiss."

HE SPEECH FOLKLORE of a nation is always a work in progress. It is continually being shaped by the unique identity of its people groups: by the way they live and the climate and geography they live in; by the food they eat and the way in which they obtain that food. New generations in their turn are always being shaped, at least in part, by the folklore that is handed down to them. They, in their turn, further shape that folklore, in a never-ending cyclical pattern in which speech and identity evolve together.

What is folklore? Kemp P. Battle says:

Folklore has always been too impatient, too spontaneous to stand still for definition. . . . Folklore is primarily, though not exclusively, an oral tradition passed from one person to another, one generation to the next. Taken as a whole, it represents a people's culture as seen through the changing prism of its stories, beliefs, legends, superstitions, and songs. Taken in its parts, folklore is as varied and unending as the people who create it.

All folklorists seem to agree that the one constant of folklore is change. According to Tristram P. Coffin and Hennig Cohen, editors of *Folklore in America,*

Folklore cannot survive in a set form. Folklore continually changes, varying and developing, because it is shaped by the memories, creative talents, and immediate needs of human beings in particular situations. This process, the process of oral

*variation, is the lifeblood of folklore. When it is halted by printing
or recording, folklore enters a state of suspended animation. It
comes alive again only when it flows back into oral circulation.*

America was known for many decades as a great "melting
pot." Immigrants brought their **indigenous** cultures here, and
while much was retained from each contributing culture, North
Americans showed a strong ability to stamp on those tales, patterns, and traditions a unique, North American imprint.

Although the widespread influence of television, radio,
movies, and videos is now beginning to dilute the uniqueness of
regional speech and mannerisms, the folk speech and folklore of
some regions are still as recognizably distinct as fingerprints.
"Y'all" remains a clear indicator of the American South, where in
some areas married women are still addressed by their first name
prefaced with a "Miss" as a sign of respect.

Different terms and dialects originate from distinct groups
working and living closely together. At first, these terms and
speech patterns may be known as **slang** or **jargon**, but after they remain in use for an extended period and begin to be employed by a
large segment of the general population, they
become a part of folk language and speech,
which successfully resists countless attempts to
"correct" it. Speech, according to Emrich, author of *Folk Language and Grammar,* is "by far
the most active, widespread, and continuing el-
ements in the field of folklore."

Jan Harold Brunvand, in *The Study of American Folklore,* says, "The easiest test of a folk
group's existence is a specialized vocabulary."
He lists several different areas of folk speech.

Language is thought incarnate;
mythology soul incarnate. The one is
the instrument of thought, the other
the essence of thought. In mythology,
language assumes personality and
independence. Often the significance
of the words becomes the essential
idea.

—Hubert Howe Bancroft

DIALECT (TRADITIONAL DEVIATION FROM STANDARD SPEECH)

Although the study of dialect (sometimes also known as "linguistic geography") is most often viewed as a part of **linguistics**, folklorists also study the dialects of different groups. They find deviations from standard speech in folktales, songs, and rhymes, and are particularly interested in the linguistic changes that take place when folklore is transmitted orally. They also study the use of outmoded dialect forms in folklore. Dialect may include several kinds of variations.

Variations of Grammar

In folk speech, this usually refers to nonstandard word forms or word order. Brunvand provides examples frequently used in regional folk speech, specifically past tense verbs such as "snew" for snowed; "seen" for saw; "clim" or "clum" for climbed; and "fotch" for fetched.

Syntactical Variations

Syntax is the way in which words are put together to form phrases, clauses, or sentences. Emrich, in *American Folklore*, pinpoints not vocabulary but syntax and usage as the chief difference between folk English and Standard English. Each form of the language has its own common syntax. Variations are immediately noticeable to listeners and often pinpoint the identity of the speaker. As examples, here are some syntactical variations often attributed to Pennsylvania Germans:

"Don't eat yourself done, there's a pie back."
"The off is on" (meaning "the vacation has begun").

"Throw Mama from the train a kiss."
"Outen the lights."

Syntactical variations like these show up most frequently in the speech of nonnative groups.

Dialect Pronunciations

Missouri is often called "Missoura" by its natives; Louisville is known as "Louieville." Most people say "Arkansaw," but the Arkansas River in Kansas is pronounced like the state it flows through. In the Scranton, Pennsylvania, area, a dialect known locally as "Valleyese" renders a town spelled Throop as "Troop" and third and three as "tird" and "tree." With is commonly pronounced "wit."

Some speakers also often add extra syllables (for instance, the word "athlete" becomes "athalete"). When specific immigrant groups mispronounce words in certain ways, folk stories and jokes sometimes grow up around these mispronunciations. The Swedish immigrants had a well-known habit of replacing "j" with "y." This gave rise to jokes about Swedes confusing "jail" with "Yale" (the Ivy League university). As Americans have become more accepting of the habits and speech patterns of

When Swedish immigrants replaced "j" with "y," the joke arose that some might confuse "jail" with "Yale."

> Speech is the most precious of our possessions, the instrument of our thoughts, the organ of our social nature, the means of our culture; its use is not daily or hourly alone, but momently; it is the first thing we learn, the last we forget; it is the most intimate and clinging of our habits, and almost a second nature.
>
> —William Dwight Whitney

people from other nations, such jokes are now usually frowned upon as demeaning and disrespectful.

Dialect Vocabulary

Linguistic geographers have done extensive mapping of regional variations in dialect vocabulary and are often able to pinpoint within a small number of miles a person's place of origin by the terms they use for certain objects. Examples include the following terms, all for the same small, reddish worm:

earthworm
angleworm
night crawler
night walker
mud worm
fish worm

The debate as to whether carbonated drinks are called soda or pop also continues, and in some areas of the South, coke is the

"Knee-deep in August."

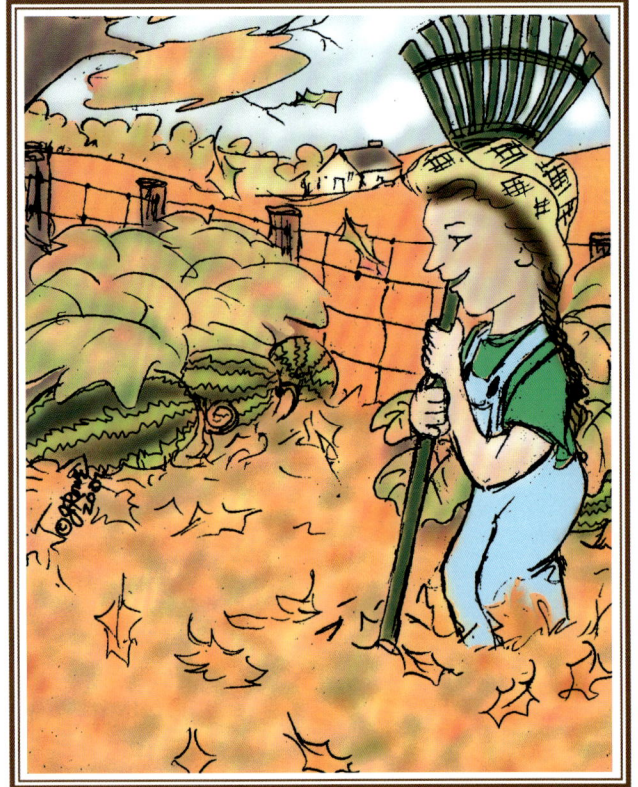

word of choice, though the word may be used for drinks other than the "real thing."

EUPHEMISMS AND INTENSIFIERS

Euphemisms and *intensifiers* are also considered a form of folk speech. Euphemisms include words used in substitution for bodily functions, feces, flatulence, and pregnancy. Intensifiers such as "hogwash!" and "oh, fudge!"

When a lawyer in southwest Missouri needed to record the exact date of a woman's death, he questioned three of her relatives. Here are the three ways in which they pinpointed the time of her sickness and death:

"just past the peak of watermelon time."
"when we was just about knee-deep in August."
"at the start of kitchen-settin' weather." (the first chilly period when people congregate around the stove inside to keep warm)

From Vance Randolph's *Down in the Holler: A Gallery of Ozark Folk Speech.*

are also part of folk speech, as are words commonly used in place of swearing (such as "drat" or "darn").

SECRET LANGUAGES

Secret languages are another form of folk speech, one that children often enjoy. These contrived languages allow children to communicate with friends, without anyone else knowing what they are saying. Here are several examples.

Pig Latin
Drop the first letter of each word, put it at the end of the word and add *ay*. Thus "She speaks pig Latin" becomes "heshay peakshay igpay atinlay."

Bop Talk
Simon Bronner, in *American Children's Follklore,* explains that when speaking this made-up language, children add *op* to each consonant but pronounce vowels normally. Unlike pig Latin, which handles each word as a whole, bop talk changes each word letter by letter. Here is Bronner's example of "Speaking bop talk is fun" translated into bop talk: "Sop pop E A kop I nop gop bop O pop top A lop kop I sop fop U nop."

Egg-Talk
This secret language involves putting the word *egg* before every vowel in each word. "Speaking egg-talk is fun" becomes "Speggeakegging eggegg teggalk eggis feggun."

FOLK OR DIALECT TERMS NOW PART OF THE GENERAL SPEECH

From the military:

KP (Kitchen Police)
SOP (Standard Operating Procedure)
no sweat
deuce and a half (a two-and-a-half-ton truck)
SNAFU (Situation Normal, All Fouled Up)

From the drug culture:

turn on
trip
speed
grass
pot

From space exploration and engineering:

A-OK
blast off
lift off
cherry picker
gantry

Ubbie Dubbie

Yet another secret language enjoyed by kids, ubbie dubbie puts a double "bb" between each pronounced vowel. "This is a weird way to talk" becomes "Thibbis ibbis abba wiebbierd wabbay toobboo tabbalk."

REGIONAL SPEECH PATTERNS

According to the *American Heritage Dictionary of the English Language* (Fourth Edition, 2000), the principal regions of American English developed during the 18th century, because it was during that period that American cultural areas took shape. "Wherever clearcut boundaries of culture can be reconstructed . . . dialect differences can be predicted based on . . . the recorded experience of the forebears of a speech community."

Northern European immigrants (primarily British, Irish, Scots, German, and Swedish) brought with them distinctive words that came to mark early North American frontier speech. These words still survive in some American Midland and South-

CB LANGUAGE

When Citizens' Band two-way radios became widely available, their use generated a new "CB language." Some of the most widely used terms and phrases follow:

the dirty side—the eastern United States
the clean side—the western United States
Smokey the Bear—highway patrolman
Smokey's in the woods taking pictures—highway patrolman checking speeds
bedbug haulers—furniture trucks
future junkyard—truck load of new cars (also known as a "portable parking lot")

ern dialects. Some of these words date all the way back to Old and **Middle English**. Included are:

- pronouns:
  hit (for it), hisn

- verbs:
  clumb, drug, holp, riz, mought could

- words also found in Robert Burns' poetry:
  duds (clothes), gumption, hunkers, mountain billy (hillbilly), chimla (chimney), het (heated), southron (southern)

Euphemisms Common to School-children:

booger	nasal mucus
goober	drool; mucus
doo-doo	feces
pee	to urinate
poop	to excrete feces

REGIONAL WORDS

Though these words were once a ready indicator of place of origin, all languages change continually, and North American English is no exception. Though many words were once limited to specific areas of the country, they may now be found throughout the country. For example, the Northern states commonly used words such as:

burlap bag
chipmunk
clapboards
faucet
fried cake (doughnut)
haycock

lobbered milk (clabbered milk)
spider (three-legged frying pan)
teeter-totter

Pennsylvania words included:

blinds (window shades)
skillet (frying pan)
green beans

Southern words included:

snack
slaw (coleslaw)
seesaw

CHARACTERISTICS OF AMERICAN FOLK SPEECH: TO BE OR NOT TO BE

In the past tense of "to be," the *were* form commonly disappears, leaving the single *was* form. Examples:

we was
you was
they was

The past participle loses the auxiliary *have*, leaving:

Where you been? I been to town.

Isn't and *aren't* become "ain't."

COLLEGE TERMS

Another group that generates its own "folkspeech" is that of college students. Course names are sometimes replaced with humorous or derogatory substitutes:

Nuts and Sluts—Abnormal Psychology
Rocks for Jocks—Introductory Geology
Tanks and Jeeps—Military History
Play a Day—English Drama

Adapted from *The Study of American Folklore*, by Jan Harold Brunvand.

To Have
Often reduced to *a,* as in "He couldn'a done it."

To Use
Often used as an adverb, as in "I use to could do that, but now I can't."

Done

Often used as an auxiliary:

  I done went into town.
  He's done gone.

Personal Pronouns
You often becomes:

Yous
yous guys
you'ns
y'all

Nowadays many people all over the country say "you guys" as a simple plural, no matter what the gender of the people addressed.

Articles
An before vowels or a silent *h* becomes *a* (sometimes with an *n* moved to the noun), so *an apple* becomes *a napple*; *an oyster* becomes *a noyster.* This common British speech pattern is still heard among the inhabitants of Newfoundland.

Redundant Subjects
The boy went to school becomes *The boy he went to school. He ought to have his head examined* becomes *Him, he ought to have his head examined.*

Double Negatives
Unlike standard English double negatives, which are commonly understood to mean a positive, double negatives in folk speech simply reinforce the negative—and are easier to pronounce as well. Examples include: *I don't need no help from you!* (which in regular grammatical usage would work out to mean the speaker needs help—but not in this usage). A well-known multiple negative from the Ozarks goes: "I ain't never done no dirt of no kind to nobody."

Language changes continually, but such changes have many different causes. In *Folk Language and Grammar*, Emrich explains that one cause is the habit people have of hearing names and

A fisherman from Nova Scotia uses a distinct vocabulary.

words "within the limits of their own vocabulary and under-standing." Emrich recounts the story of a guest on a 1970 TV talk show who referred twice to a man as being "flustrated." He suggests that the woman might have already known the word "frustrated," heard someone use the word "flustered," and hearing it within her own limits, somehow come up with the hybrid "flustrated." He uses similar examples for "the blunt end of it," an obvious variation of "the brunt of it," and for the phrase "to wet the apptite," instead of "to whet the appetite."

Folk naming, another important form of folk speech, is such a large category that the next chapter will deal solely with that subject.

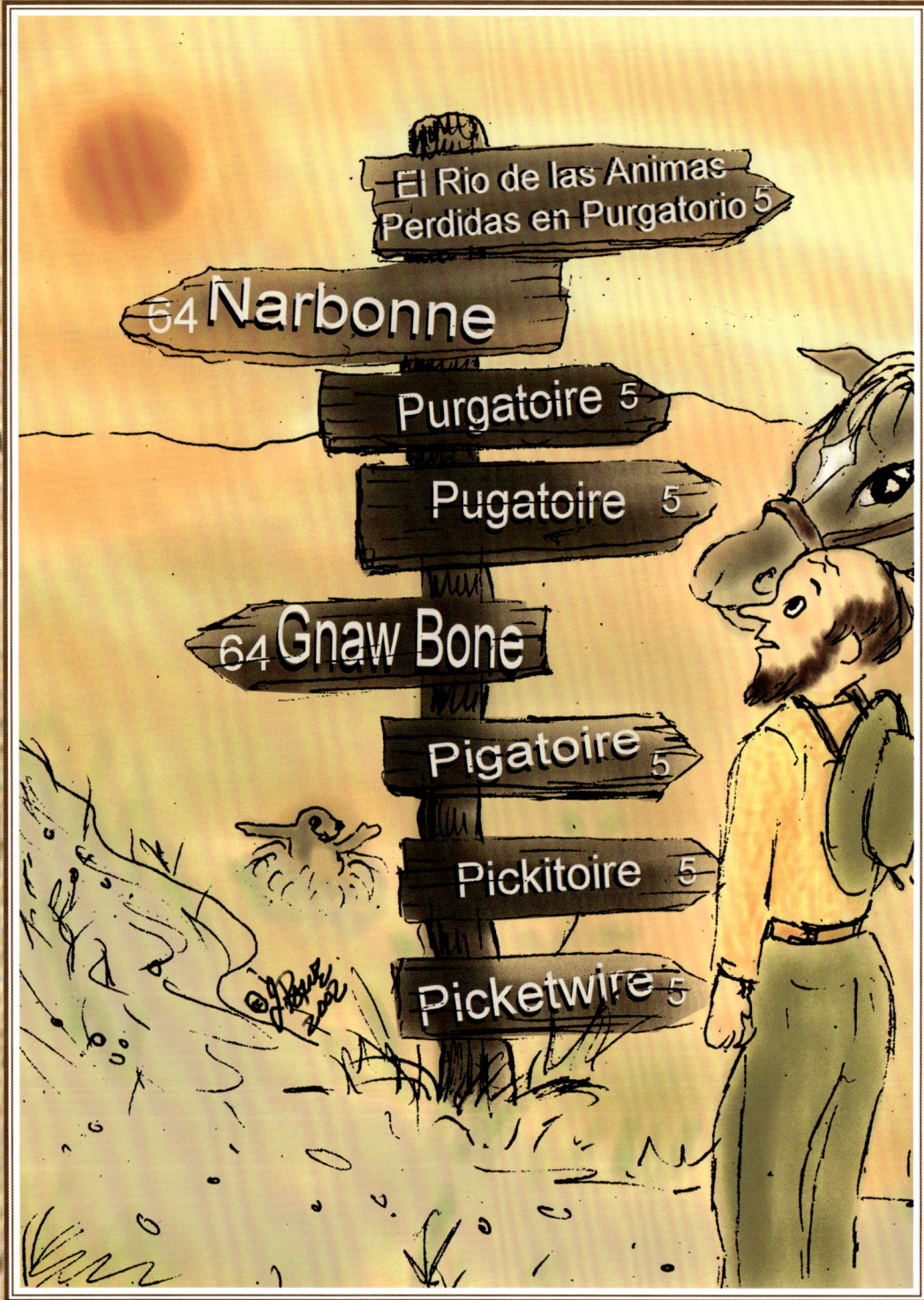

El Rio de las Animas
Perdidas en Purgatorio 5

54 Narbonne

Purgatoire 5

Pugatoire 5

64 Gnaw Bone

Pigatoire 5

Pickitoire 5

Picketwire 5

The names of some places have a long history.

TWO

Names
A Story in a Word

According to legend, when Spanish explorers searching for gold first landed on Canada, they said, "Aca nada" ("Nothing there"), creating the name "Canada."

A SMALL BAND of about 30 Spanish explorers traveled north from Mexico into the American Southwest, where they were killed by enemy Native Americans on the bank of the lower Colorado River. The explorers had no priest with them and so died without absolution. When explorers later found the skeletons of the unfortunate men, they did what was common at that time: they named the place in honor of the terrible event that had taken place there, calling it El Rio de las Animas Perdidas en Purgatorio, which means the River of the Souls Lost in Purgatory.

Eventually, French trappers traveled across the land and shortened the unmanageable name to Purgatoire, and that is how it is listed on maps today. However, the river gained a folk name when people from Kentucky and Texas heard the name and, not reconizing the French, changed it from Purgatoire to Pugatoire to Pigatoire to Pigitoire to Pickitoire to Picketwire—a word with which they were familiar.

A similar story happened with a French frontier town in Indiana called Gnaw Bone. When westward-moving Kentuckians, who had never heard of the French town Narbonne, came across a town with that name near Bloomington, Indiana, they heard Gnaw Bone, words they could understand. And so the town is named today.

The study of names is a subject in itself, called **onomastics**, but folklorists find much to mine from the meaning and use of names for people, places, and things.

NAMES FOR PEOPLE

A common practice in North American culture is to name children after a notable man or woman. For instance, many boys named George Washington have turned up throughout America's history since the time of the first United States president, including George Washington Carver (1864–1943), the famous America botanist, and George Washington Gale Ferris, inventor of the Ferris Wheel, first unveiled at the 1893 Chicago World's Fair.

Nicknames, on the other hand, are often chosen on the basis of appearance or behavior. Nicknames can come from many sources, including:

- common shortening of a name (Dick, Joe, Peg)

- occupation (Butch, Teach, Cookie)
  Some examples of these nicknames include Louis the Barber, Sailor Jack, Dan the Paper Hanger, Garbage Mike, Butcher John, and Bedbug Smith (the exterminator for boardinghouses near Virginia City, Nevada).

- place of origin (Tex, Mex, Nevada)
  Names from place of origin included Telluride Joe, Frisco Kate, and Dublin Dan. Names from country of origin included China Charlie, Nick the Greek, Spanish Joe, Frenchy, and Swede.

- physical characteristics (Red, Shorty)
  Children often bestow cruel nicknames in this category—like Fatty, Skinny, Four-Eyes, Dummy, Pimples—but these nicknames seldom last. Other descriptive names seem

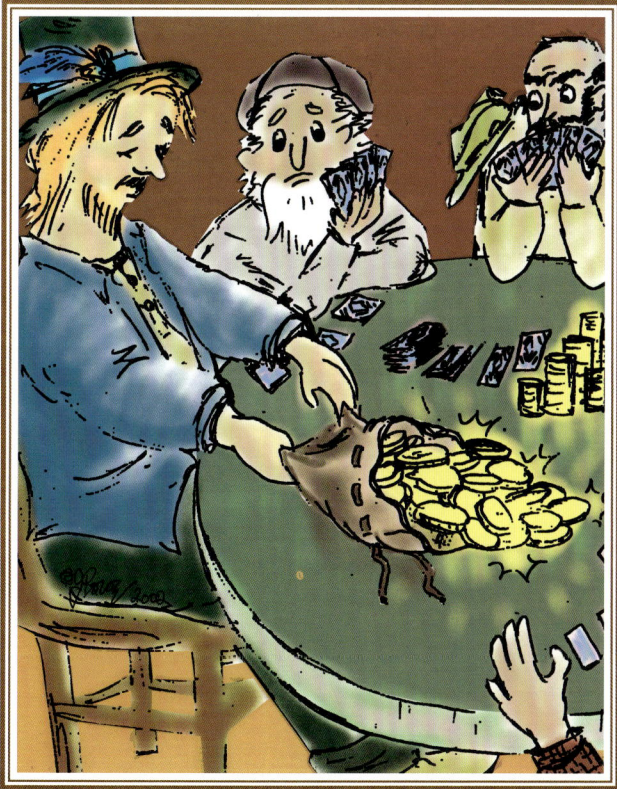

Hundred-Dollar Jim always wagered a hundred dollars.

to stick with people throughout their lives: Crooked-Nose Pete, One-Eyed Murphy, and Dirty-Face Jack are examples. Some nicknames are "earned," such as Peg-Leg Annie, whose feet were frozen in a snowstorm and had to be amputated with a meat saw and jackknife. (Frontier folklore records that her only form of painkiller was whiskey, after which she was tied down for the operation.)

- unusual events, actions, or peculiarities
    Unsinkable Mrs. Brown arrived in Colorado after surviving the sinking of the *Titanic*; Hundred-Dollar Jim never bet more than once a day, but always wagered a hundred dollars in gold. Sometimes people were described in fantastic ways rather than given a nickname, such as the person who was supposedly "so cross-eyed that when he wept the tears ran down his back."

- for miscellaneous reasons (example: mispronunciation of a name: Salga for Sally, Slitch for Richard)
    When Carl Sandburg asked General Eisenhower where the name "Ike" came from, Eisenhower replied, "All of us, oddly enough, were called Ike. All the brothers. One of us

Unsinkable Mrs. Brown survived the Titanic.

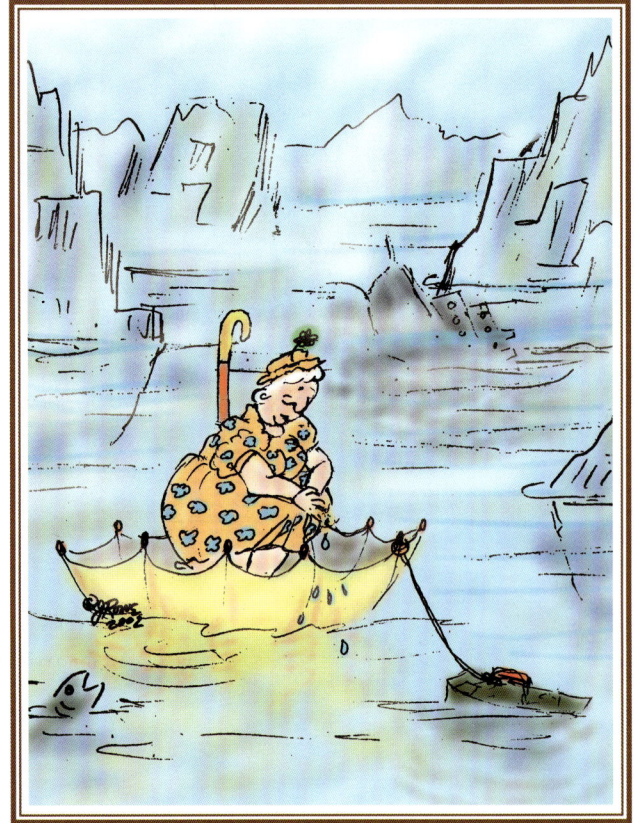

was Ugly Ike, another Big Ike. I was Red Ike, because of my red face. The others outgrew the nickname, but mine always stuck, and it was one of the luckiest things that could have happened to me. A soldier always likes a good name for his officers and generals. When they called me Uncle Ike, or during the war just plain Ike, I knew that everything was going well."

NAMES FOR PLACES

Many writers have enthused about the beauty of American place names such as Mississippi, Monogahela, Shenandoah, Manassas, Appomattox, Antietam, Philadelphia, Salem, and Chattanooga. But Robert Louis Stevenson said it best in *Across the Plains in 1892*:

There is no part of the world where **nomenclature** *is so rich, poetical, humorous, and picturesque as the United States of America. All times, races and languages have brought their contribution. Pekin is in the same State with Euclid, with Bellfontaine,* *and with Sandusky. The names of the States themselves form a chorus of sweet and most romantic vocables: Delaware, Ohio, Indiana, Florida, Dakota, Iowa, Wyoming, Minnesota, and the Carolinas: there are few poems with a nobler music for the ear: a songful, tuneful land.*

Places are named in different ways. One of the most common is to name a place after people, usually founders or settlers, or to name it in honor of some historically important person, often a military personage. The second most common method of place naming is to use a name from the Old World, often preceding it with "New." The third way of naming includes describing the land for easy remembrance and recognition by those who will come later: Sierra Nevada (snowy mountain range), El Rio Grande (the big river), Las Vegas (the plains), or Detroit (the narrows). Spanish and French explorers named places for important

ORIGINAL PLACE NAMES IN APPALACHIA

Black Rock	Broken Leg
Standing Stone	Raw Dough
Sharp Top	Gouge-eye
Twenty Mile	Vengeance
Naked Place	Chunky Gal
The Pocket	Rip Shin Thicket
Tumbling Creek	Dog-hobble Ridge
Mad Sheep Mountain	Devil's Racepath
Dog Slaughter Creek	Greasy Creek

members of the Catholic faith, including San or Santa in the name, the words for saint or holy: Santa Barbara, San Diego, San Francisco, Santa Cruz. Other names are drawn from the ancient world, including Rome, Corinth, Athens, and Utica.

Strongly folk-based names sometimes describe the geography of the countryside:

Camelback Mountain
Sugar Loaf Mountain
Rabbit Ears Pass
Grand Junction (at the meeting of the Gunnison and
    Colorado Rivers)
Chimney Rock
the Coffeepot (a large, freestanding rock
    shaped like its name)
Blue River

Folk names can also describe the animals and plants that live in the area

Coyote Wells
Lone Pine
Blueberry Hill
Wildcat Hollow
Moosehead Lake
Chestnut Grove

How many geographical spots can you recognize, using the names listed above?

In the town of Elkader you'll need to watch out for carnivorous elks!

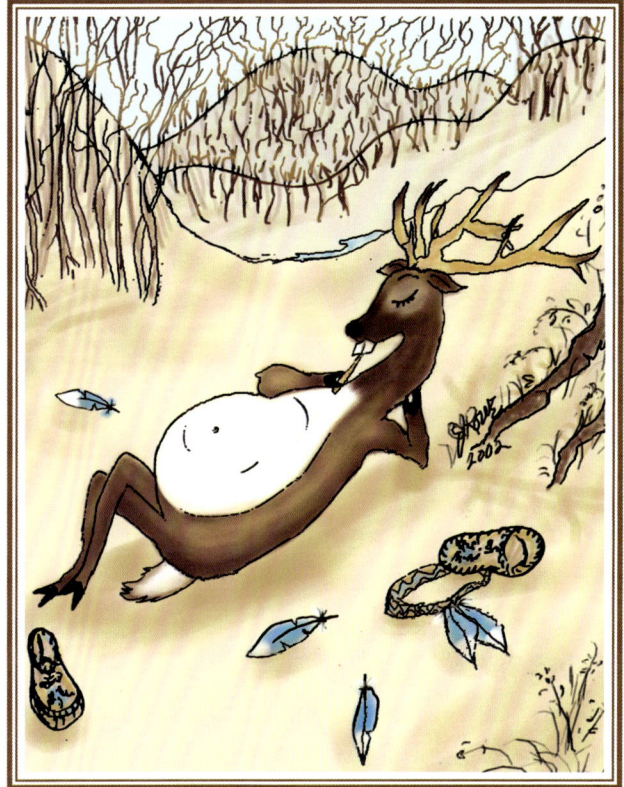

In addition, place names may refer to noteworthy events that occurred or objects that were found there:

Massacre Lake
Skull Valley
Burnt Ranch
Deadman Gap

Other stories of how the beautiful and interesting names of North America came to be, however, are often more fascinating than the names themselves, as in the story of the Picketwire River.

Some stories of place names seem to be made up after the fact, as in the name for Elkader, a town in northeastern Iowa.

In the first version of the story, Abt El Kader, who did deeds of great bravery in remote Africa, gave his name to the town to ensure that it would become a place where courage lived.

In the second version, the Native Americans who lived there centuries ago had among them a little girl who was their princess and their greatest treasure. She loved the beautiful setting and lovely hills that surrounded the village. But the chief warned her again and again that she must never go up into the hills alone.

One day, however, the sunlight shone brightly on all the trees and the wind made their leaves and branches dance, enticing the princess to break the chief's command. Although she did not mean to disobey, she wandered high into the hills. And there, an *elk ate her.* If you doubt this story and reply that elks are not carnivorous, the Native Americans will point to the hills in November, when every leaf has been stripped from every tree. In such a cruel environment, they will ask, is it any wonder that even an elk could learn to eat human flesh?

Other place name stories are plain and down to earth, as in the simple explanation given for the name of Justus, a tiny hamlet in Northeastern Pennsylvania. "Just us," the people there explain to visitors. "The name means exactly what it says—*just us.*"

Canada has colorful place names as well,

names that grew out of the country's mixture of Native American, French, Scottish, Irish, Greek, Spanish, German, Italian, and English heritage. Names taken from the country's past history include:

Frontenac
Cartier
Victoria
Carleton
Charlottestown
Dorchester

Other names are linked to local legends, including:

Moose Jaw, or the place-where-the-white-man-mended-his-
    cart-with-the-jawbone-of-a-moose
Kicking Horse Pass, a pass in the Rockies where a doctor
    was kicked by his horse while exploring
Medicine Hat, where two Native Americans fought, with
    the Cree medicine man losing his headdress to a Blackfoot

The name Canada itself, according to one legend, resulted from the cry of Spanish sailors who did not find the gold they expected and said "Aca nada," or *nothing here*.

Canada also has names for people from various regions of the country, including:

Bluenose for Nova Scotia
Herring-Choker for New
    Brunswick

Peasouper for Quebec
Bison for Manitoba
Spud Islander for Prince Edward Island
Newfie for Newfoundland

NAMES FOR THINGS AND EVENTS

Unusual names for the ordinary things people use and handle abound in folk speech. The importance of money in everyday life is apparent from the number of words used to refer to it

beans
chips
checks
dope
dust
flimsey
lead
meaks-kim (Blackfoot)
needful
queer (counterfeit)
rocks
root
scads
stamps
shinnias (Cree)

otter-skins
the velvet

Food, another essential, comes under the term "grub," for everything that's edible. Other more specific folk words include:

dope (butter)
dough-gods (dumplings)
tin-cow (condensed milk)
tent-pegs (frozen beefsteak cut into strips for use in the camps)
baked-wind-pills (Boston baked beans)
mountain oysters (calves fries).

Important life events were often spoken of with folk expressions. Dying was called "crossing the great divide," "passing in his checks," or "moving over the range." One Native American tribe called it "going to the sand-hills."

Much of North American folk speech has a tongue-in-cheek quality. Such is the case in describing a man who got married as "hitched" or "hobbled."

Primitive cultures saw the name of a person, place, or thing as being intimately and tangibly connected to the true essence of that person or object; a person often kept his or her true name a secret, as a way of protecting the deepest life force. In the biblical book of Genesis, when Adam names

The name of this town in Texas implies something greater than mere size.

creation, names were a means of exercising control over the created world. Naming practices continued to play an important role in the folklore of North Americans. Names help us shape our world. They give us a handle by which we can grab hold of reality.

Davy Crockett owed much of his fame to his powerful speech.

THREE

The Power of
Persuasion
Politics, Boasts, and
"Speechifying"

Scheherazade saved her life with her fascinating stories.

THROUGHOUT HISTORY, most cultures have honored and followed people who speak well. From as far back as 3400 BC comes this advice from Ptahhotep:

Be a craftsman in speech that thou mayest be strong, for the strength of one is the tongue, and speech is mightier than all fighting.

From the ancient tale of "The Thousand and One Nights," in which Scheherazade must tell the king a new story every night to save her own life, to the debate clubs in American high schools today, the value we put upon speaking fluently and persuasively is evident.

The fascination of Americans with bigger-than-life heroes is nowhere more evident than in the history of the nation's politics; political power was intertwined with the ability to speak well. In the case of Davy Crockett, who first went to the Tennessee state legislature in 1821, his speeches seem to be a combination of **hyperbole**, confidence, and hair-raising narrative, but they won him a considerable following. Crockett made the following speech during an extended controversy with another legislator over the passage of a bill:

*Mr. Speaker—Do you know what that man's bill reminds me of? Well, Il'spose you don't, so I'll tell you. Well, Mr. Speaker, when I first come to this country, a blacksmith was a rare thing; but there happened to be one in my neighborhood: he had no **striker**, and whenever one of the neighbors wanted any work done, he had to*

In the famous Mid-Eastern collection of tales known as "The Arabian Nights" (or "The Thousand and One Nights"), Sultan Schahriar is convinced that all women are faithless, so he decides to have each of his wives put to death after their first night together. The Sultana Scheherazade was creative and clever enough to save her life by getting him interested in the stories she told him for one thousand and one nights. She was such a powerful speaker that he kept postponing her execution. Eventually, he decided he would let her live.

go over and strike till his work was finished. These were hard times, Mr. Speaker, but we had to do the best we could.

It happened that one of my neighbors wanted an axe, so he took along with him a piece of iron, and went over to the blacksmith's to strike till his axe was done. The iron was heated, and my neighbor fell to work, and was striking there nearly all day; when the blacksmith concluded the iron wouldn't make an axe, but 'twould make a fine mattock. So my neighbor wanting a mattock, concluded he would go over and strike till his mattock was done. Accordingly, he went over the next day, and worked faithfully; but toward night the blacksmith concluded his iron wouldn't make a mattock but 'twould make a fine ploughshare. So my neighbor wanting a ploughshare, agreed that he would go over the next day and strike till that was done. Accordingly, he again went over and fell hard to work; but towards night the blacksmith concluded his iron wouldn't make a ploughshare, but 'twould make a fine skow. So my neighbor, tired of working, cried, "A skow let it be." And the blacksmith taking up the red hot iron, threw it into a trough of water near him, and as it fell in, it sung out "skow."

And this, Mr. Speaker, will be the way with that man's bill for a county. He'll keep you all here doing nothing, and finally his bill will turn out a skow, now mind if it don't.

This speech was published in 1833 in the book *The Life and Adventures of Colonel David Crockett of West Tennessee* (reprinted that year as *Sketches and Eccentricities of Col. David Crockett of West Tennessee*), and according to Richard M. Dorson, in *American in Legend; Folklore from the Colonial Period to the Present*, it "solidified Crockett's reputation as a character and an 'original.'" Dorson comments on Crockett's narration style, which became an integral part of his political technique. He would give his listeners a good "yarn" to relax them and in this way catch their attention, and then sometimes apply the moral of his tale to the political issue at hand, a technique Lincoln would later use with even greater effectiveness.

A new kind of American folk hero was being formed during this era—one "sprung from the people," writes Dorson, "participating actively in the democratic process, and larding his speeches with jokes, stories, and salty sayings in the popular idiom, rather than in pompous rhetoric, to win support for his issues. In short order Crockett became a subject as well as a vendor of humorous tales."

The tough, independent mindedness of the American pioneer was drawn to men like David Crockett, who seemed to them to be "one of our own kind." He had little schooling, but depended on "natural-born sense instead of law learning." He didn't quote legal precedents to support his position, but instead used proverbs that his constituents could grasp easily. As a politician, Crockett seems to have fostered this image of himself through his storytelling. In *Sketches and Eccentricities,* the author comments that "While electioneering, the colonel always conciliates every crowd into which he may be thrown by the narration of some anecdote"; "He has lived almost entirely in the woods, and his life has been a continued scene of anecdote to one fond of hairbreadth escapes and hunting stories"; "He was ever the humorous hero of his own story. . . . "As Crockett portrayed himself triumphing in various situations involving bears and panthers and even human opponents, he made himself more attractive to the people as a strong and able candidate for political office.

As a man of the people, he was plainly dressed and plain spoken, and his constituents loved his image as a "product of forests, freedom, universal suffrage, and bear-hunts." The story is told that, when he was ridiculed by a fashionably dressed legislator for his own plain dressing, Crockett pinned a cambric ruffle torn from the shirt of the well-dressed lawmaker to his own coarse shirt. When he made his appearance this way in the House, the entire place dissolved into laughter and sided with Crockett and his insistence on his democratic right to be exactly who he was. Crockett's speeches and tales soon became legendary for their

TALKING MATCH

An old story tells of a talking match in New Orleans. It was said to go on for 13 hours, with a Frenchman and a Kentuckian doing the talking. The bystanders and judges were talked to sleep, and when they woke in the morning, they found the Frenchman dead and the Kentuckian whispering in his ear.

Adapted from *Great American Folklore*, compiled by Kemp P. Battle.

backwoods flavor, and versions of them are recorded in *Twenty-Five Cents Worth of Nonsense; or, The Treasure Box of Unconsidered Trifles* (1873) and *Davy Crockett's Almanac of Wild Sports in the West, Life in the Backwoods, & Sketches of Texas* (1837).

DAVY CROCKETT'S ELECTION SPEECH

One day, when I was getting ready to go down into Green Swamp for a mess of rattlesnakes, Luke Wing, Grizzle Newcome, and Batt Wiggle cum to my house to try to coax me to set up for Congress. I told them I didn't understand them kind of splunctifications; but they told me it was sartain the country would be ruined if I didn't go to Congress. So I seed thar war no other way, and so I got ready to go round among the 'lectors, and argufy upon it. I went down to Hay Hollow and ketched a pesky great alligator, and made a bridle for him of painter's hides, and then I got on his back, and rid up to Bear Cleering, whar thar war a whole heap of fellows talking politicks. I driv rite in among 'em, and my crockodile opened his mouth as wide as Black Cave, and they war all astonished. It did wonders for my election. When he opened his mouth every tooth in his head counted for a voter, and when I driv through 'em, I yelled seven times as loud as a hull drove of injins, and then I crowed till my eyes stuck out two inches. T'other candidate begun to think he had a smart chance of losing his 'lections; so he got on the stump to speechify. But I driv my alligator right up to the spot, and he opened his mouth

could detect a man who would steal horses from his neighbors." The jury was so impressed, they found the defendant not guilty. The lawyer ran for state office. When asked afterward if he had really stolen the horses, the defendant hesitated before he answered. "I sure thought I did, but after hearin' that speech, I'll be danged if I know fer sure."

In 1937, a story appeared in the *Saturday Evening Post* titled "The Devil and Daniel Webster," by Stephen Vincent Benét, and was soon hailed as an American classic. It had the feel of a folk legend and seemed to be on a plane with "The Legend of Sleepy Hollow" and the stories of Rip Van Winkle or Huckleberry Finn. Although the story is literature rather than folklore, it accurately reflects the folklore of 19th-century North America. "The Devil and Daniel Webster" is a fine example of the awe—almost reverence—early Americans felt toward men who were "well-spoken." Because of his speaking ability, Daniel Webster, a historical character in the fictional story, was a real-life North American hero.

In Benét's story, an unsuccessful New Hampshire farmer named Jabez Stone bemoans his troubles by saying, "I vow it's enough to make a man want to sell his soul to the devil! And I would, too, for two cents!"

Though nothing happened at that moment, by the next day the Devil appeared to close the bargain. For the next seven years, Jabez prospers at everything he touches, even to the point of becoming a state senator, and "the Stone family was as happy and contented as cats in a dairy."

Except for Jabez, that is, who knew the

According to the fictional account, Daniel Webster was such a fluent speaker that he won an argument with the devil himself.

day of reckoning was coming. When he witnesses the terrifying sight of the Devil collecting the soul of his neighbor, Miser Stevens, Jabez hurries to get help from Daniel Webster.

Webster loses his first verbal battles with the Devil and, as a lawyer, calls for a proper trial by a jury of the Devil's choice, just as long as they're all Americans.

Benét describes Stone's fear upon seeing the jury—twelve of the most vile and hated Americans recalled from their place in Hell—this way: "If Jabez Stone had been sick with terror before, he was blind with terror now." As Daniel Webster sees the jurors enter and recognizes what terrible men they were in their lifetimes, as he encounters the Devil's unfair practices as "judge," he

The historical Daniel Webster.

begins "to heat, like iron in the forge." He intends to burst out with "lightnings and denunciations," then realizes that fighting such evil men with their own weapons would cause him to fall into their power.

Webster wisely changes his tactics, gets to his feet, and begins with

the simple things that everybody's known and felt—the fresh-ness of a fine morning when you're young, and the taste of food when you're hungry, and the new day that's every day when you're a child. He took them up and he turned them in his hands. They were good things for any man. But without free-

dom, they sickened. . . . And he wasn't pleading for any one person any more, though his voice rang like an organ. He was telling the story and the failures and the endless journey of mankind. . . . And his words came back at the end to New Hampshire ground, and the one sport of land that each man loves and clings to . . . and to each one of that jury he spoke of things long forgotten. For his voice could search the heart, and that was his gift and his strength. And to one, his voice was like the forest and its secrecy, and to another like the sea and the storms of the sea and one heard the cry of his lost nation in it, and another saw a little harmless scene he hadn't remembered for years.

When at last Webster finishes his speech, a surprising verdict is rendered. Walter Butler rises to pronounce the verdict in favor of Jabez Stone and adds, "even the damned may salute the eloquence of Mr. Webster."

But even then Webster is not finished. He makes the "long-barreled, slab-sided, lantern-jawed, fortune-telling note shaver" Devil promise to never bother any other New Hampshire man till doomsday, and the Devil agrees.

In the ongoing search for a bigger-than-life personage who could talk his way out of any trouble, Daniel Webster became the ultimate hero. The person who could speak well had earned the right to power and prestige.

In the 21st century, politicians no longer depend as heavily on their speaking skills. High-cost marketing campaigns can cre-

Today's politicians still rely on the power of their voice.

ate public images for political candidates, allowing people with meager speaking skills to run for office. But speech and politics have not been completely divorced. (For instance, Senators use the filibuster to hold up events in their favor by talking on and on and on. . . .) The folk traditions that shaped North American politics still have power.

Flower sellers had their own distinctive calls to advertise their wares.

FOUR

Buying and Selling
The Roots of Advertising

In the 18th and 19th centuries, newspaper sellers had unique street cries.

LONG BEFORE Madison Avenue perfected the art of the television commercial, and before billboards sprang up by the side of nearly every road in America, the most immediate form of advertising was the street cry.

In New Orleans, people who walked the streets could hear:

Oyster Man! Oyster Man!
Get your fresh oysters from the Oyster Man!
Bring out your pitcher, bring out your can,
Get your nice fresh oysters from the Oyster Man!

In New York, potential customers were greeted with:

'Ta-toes!
Peach-es!
'N cents a basket!

Street cries were a means to sell all sorts of staples in season, from oysters to sweet potatoes, and though some of the cries may seem hard to understand in the 21st century, they were clear to the city inhabitants of that era.

The purpose of the street cry was to advertise the wares available, and each vendor customized his own cry as far as length and style. Some cries were shouted, some chanted, some sung. In *Folklore on the American Land*, by Duncan Emrich, the author comments on the different produce and wares offered in American cities. According to the author, watermelons were "as normal

Charcoal by the bushel, charcoal by the peck. . .

date, a hand bell was to be rung as the vendor cried:

> *Charcoal by the bushel,*
> *Charcoal by the peck,*
> *Charcoal by the frying pan,*
> *Or any way you lek!*

Services were also offered by means of street cries, chiefly scissor grinding, umbrella mending, and chimney sweeping. In New Orleans, customers might hear:

> *Sweep 'em clean! Sweep 'em clean!*
> *Save the fireman lots of work,*
> *We hate soot, we never shirk,*
> *Sweep 'em clean! Sweep 'em clean!*

Some street cries were the product of an individual's personal "advertising campaign," but others were actually ordered by the local government. In the mid-1600s, Boston selectmen ordered the appointed chimneysweepers Robert Wyatt and William Lane to "cry aboutt streetes that they may be knowne." In 1686, the New York Mayor ordered chimneysweeper William Butler "to passe through all the streetes, Lanes

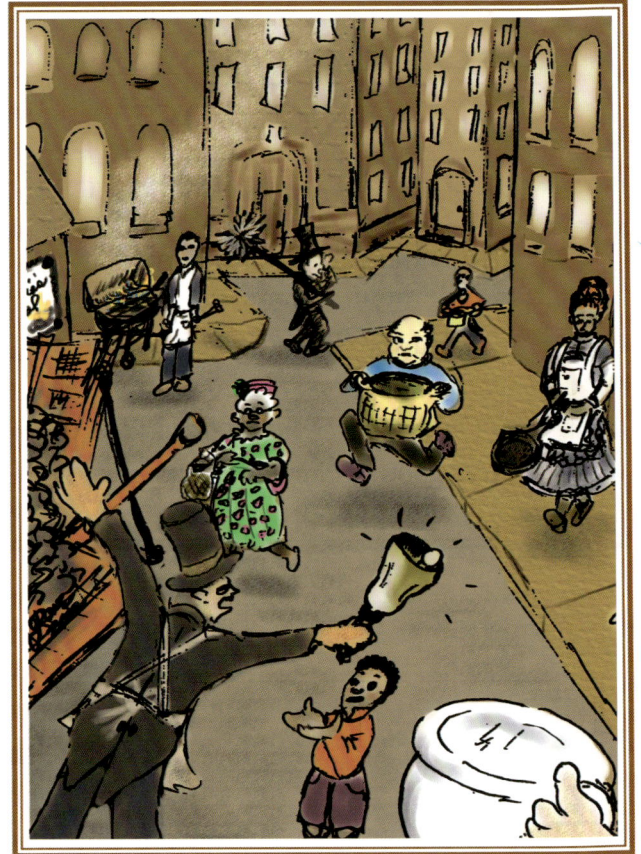

THE CRAB AND DEVILED CRAB STREET CRY

(from Baltimore)

Ah, I have 'em hot,
Ah, I have 'em brown,
Ah, I have 'em long,
Ah, I have 'em roun',
Dey's nice en fat, dey weight a poun',
Daibble!

Da-aibble! Debble, Daibble Crab!
My ol' man makes me mad,
Sen's po' me out widde Develish Crab!

Hard fried, crab cakes, en daibble crabs!
Hard fried, er yawl wide!
Crab-by Crab!

Keep yo' haid levvul!
Tom de devvul!
Ah on'y has de kin' de ladies oughter buy.
Ef yo' don' come soon ah'm ergoin' by.
Daibble! Debble Crab!
Crab-man's goin' 'way—Good-bye!

A basket seller would call out what he had to sell as he drove his wagon down city streets.

like—ague bitters—Shaker herbs—essences, winter green, peppermint, lobely—tapes, pins, needles, hooks and eyes—broaches and basslets—smelling bottles—castor ile—corn-plaster—mustard—gardning seeds—silver spoons—pocket combs—tea pots—green tea—saleratus —tracts, songbooks—thimbles—babies' whistles—copybooks, slates, playin' cards—puddin-sticks—butter-prints—baskets—wooden bowls . . . .

Later in American history, people peddled cosmetics, brushes, vacuum cleaners, encyclopedia sets, and a variety of other products from house to house, and entire companies were founded and flourished upon the services of these "door-to-door salesmen."

The street cry, though long dead in the cities of North America, can still be heard echoing at stadiums around the country during baseball season, as vendors pass through the stands crying their wares:

A seller drew customers to his street cart with the persuasive power of his speech.

"Ice cold Pepsi!"

"Hot dogs!"

"Hot pretzels!"

"Beer!"

Even the cats were fascinated
by this street seller.

Sometimes a joke is the only way people can deal with disaster—like grasshoppers eating all their crops.

FIVE

Jokes
Coping with the World with Laughter

"I guess I'll float a little further!"

JOKES ARE ONE way people deal with difficult experiences, trying acquaintances, and the unfairness of life in general. North American folklore includes countless jokes in each of these categories, plus many more that are "just for fun" and the pleasure of laughter.

Jokes can also portray the character of a people. When the United States and Canada were still young countries, people went West in search of a better life. For some, this meant free land; for others, a better climate. Some even dreamed of finding gold. But a large number found the difficulties of moving west to be more than they had dreamed. One way of dealing with the painful disillusionment was to make jokes about it, and a stoical humor grew up as part of the pioneer's arsenal of "grit, grace, and gumption" necessary for surviving in an untamed land.

Pests that devoured crops (grown at great cost in human labor from painstakingly-cleared land) were a special threat. The stoical humor needed to deal with these losses is evident in the story of the grasshopper who "ate the farmer's team of mules and then pitched the horseshoes for the wagon" and in this quote from Nebraska, where the farmer could stand by his field and hear the grasshoppers devouring the crop:

Grasshoppers on the potato vines eat downward, and when they come to a potato bug, they kick it calmly and go on their devastating way.

Jokes were (and still are) often made in the form of sly comments about another person's character. Certain occupations,

73

such as lawyer, were targeted with jokes far more than others. The following story is an example:

When two men passed a tombstone that read "Here lies Sam Jones, an honest man and a good lawyer," one man remarked to the other, "Isn't it unusual for one grave to hold three people?"

From the beginning of North American history, people have taken great pride in their own area of residence. This pride has led to many jokes about the inability of other states to measure up as possible residences. For example, Hoosiers (people from Indiana) often tell jokes about Kentuckians, while Kentuckians frequently tell Hoosier jokes. The feelings between New York and New Jersey are evident in this joke:

When a ship went down off the Carolina coast, the captain was the only survivor. He clung to a piece of wood from the ship for several days until a local fishing boat finally spotted him. When the fishermen pulled alongside and threw him a rope, the cold, bedraggled, starving captain called, "Where am I?"

"New Jersey," the fishermen call back.

The captain gripped his piece of wood with resignation and shouted, "I guess I'll float on a little further."

Much has been written about the difficult and often tragic relationship between American settlers and Native Americans.

Davy Crockett's tame bear.

Even in such a setting, jokes have also sur-faced—some in favor of one side, some in favor of the other. In the following joke, it's easy to see the sly humor, which at first seems targeted at one group (and at politicians, too, another favorite target of traditional jokes); the end, however, surprises the listener with a sudden twist.

Some folklore humor takes the form of stories, often told with a straight face. This is a story made famous by David Crockett:

The creturs of the forest is of different kinds, like humans. Some is stupid and some is easy to larn. The most knowing cretur that ever I seed war a barr that my darter Pinetta picked up in the woods. It used to follow her to church, and at last it got so tame, it would cum into the house, and set down in one corner of the fire-place to warm itself. I larned it to smoke a pipe and while it sot in one corner smoking, I sot in the other with my pipe. We couldn't talk to one another; but we would lookd, and I knowed by the shine of his eye what he wanted to say, though he didn't speak a word. The cretur would set up o'nights when I war out late, and open the door for me. But it war the greatest in churning butter. It did all that business for the family. At last it got so civilized that it caught the hooping cough and died. My wife went to the minister and tried to get him to give the barr a christian burial: but the skunk war so bigotted that he wouldn't do it, and I told him the barr war a better christian than he ever war.

When an Oklahoman decided to run for Congress, he knew he had to get the many Indian farmers in that area on his side. He got them together and spoke to them about how the government had treated them unfairly in the past, and promised it would never happen again if he was elected. "No siree! Not in my district! I'm going to see that every one of you fellows has got a good house, and fine furniture, and a new cook stove, and an electric ice-box if he wants it."

The Indians clapped their hands and hollered "Oolah! Oolah!"

The politician was delighted at their enthusiasm and went on to promise them farms and new cars and roads without mud holes.

Again the audience clapped and hollered "Oolah! Oolah!" as loudly as they could.

Next the politician promised better livestock, both cattle and horses. The Indians went wild for the next five minutes, clapping one another on the back and hollering "Oolah! Oolah!" and the candidate was ecstatic at the reception he was receiving. On his was back into town, the candidate stopped at a large ranch where the rancher wanted to show him a prize bull worth ten thousand dollars.

Impressed at the sight of the bull, the candidate started to walk into the pen, but an Indian ranch hand touched his arm. "Come around to the other side where the pen's been cleaned up, Mister," he said. "You don't want to get oolah on your shoes."

When new inventions came along, such as electricity (with electric lights and refrigeration), telephones, and cars, they came in for their share of jokes, too. The sight of a steam train was an-

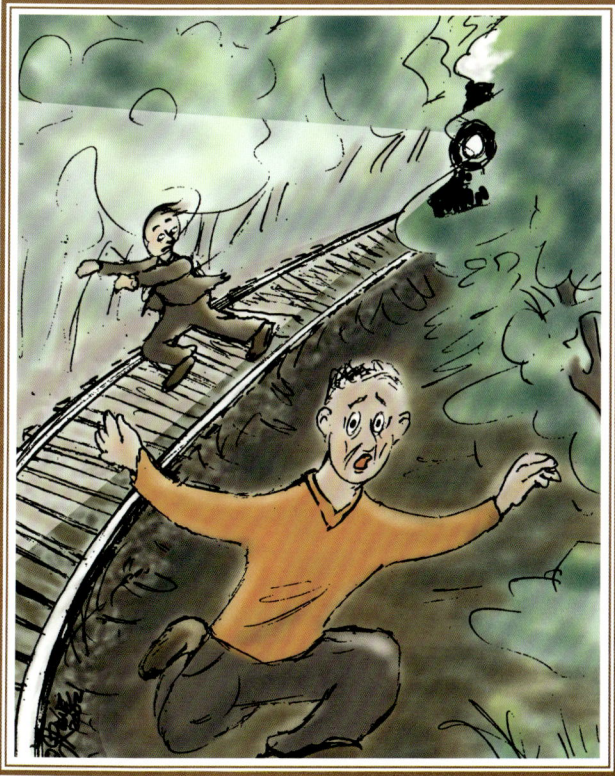

If you can't outrun a train on "this here perty road," how can you outrun it in the woods?

other occasion that seemed to inspire many jokes. "Racing the Train" is one of the best known:

Two men who had never seen a train before decided they'd go and have a look at one. Once they got there, the only things they could see were the two long, shiny rails. They lay down to wait and soon heard the awful noise of the approaching train, "the most fearsome, smoke-belchin'" thing they'd ever seen.

Frightened, they began to run ahead of the train—one along the track, the other off into the woods. Then the first man yelled to his buddy, "Bob, if I cain't outrun this thing on this here perty road, you ain't never gonna outrun it in them woods!"

Knock-knock jokes have been, and still remain, a fixture in the joke repertoire of children. In *And Other Neighborly Names*, R. Jordan points out that these jokes center around "code switching on the juvenile level," and are "generally concerned with names and naming. The joke teller pretends to introduce and name himself, but the humor resides in the fact that the 'name' turns out to be not a name at all."

Jordan speculates that the humor in knock-knock jokes is the result of two things: the delight children take in making fun of serious social customs such as introductions, and the unease they must address about their own changing self-identity.

Knock-knock.
Who's there?
Harry.
Harry who?
Harry up and open the door, it's cold out here!

Knock, knock.
Who's there?
Doughnut.
Doughnut who?
Doughnut talk to strangers knocking at your door.

Other children's joke categories include joking questions (*What did one wall say to the other wall?—I'll meet you at the corner*), elephant jokes, moron jokes, Mary Jane jokes (a specific kind of moron joke), and ethnic jokes. This last category is perhaps the most interesting to look at in detail.

Children are not the only ones to tell ethnic jokes. Simon Bronner, in *American Children's Folklore,* points out that jokes directed at those of Polish descent came into style after the Second World War, when Poland's military response to Hitler's attack was perceived as backward. "Performance in war became a test of na-

tional character," Bronner comments. During the 1960s, America's ethnic tensions rose to a peak, and once again the ethnic joke became an indicator of the strife between groups and—as some viewed jokes about African Americans—a throwback to prejudice in a time when the country was struggling to move away from prejudice. America's anger at Iran after the hostage crisis of the late 1970s was mirrored in "Iranian jokes," unknown until that time.

Canada has its own jokes, including the Pat and Mike jokes from Nova Scotia, collected by Arthur Huff Fauset in 1929. Edith Fowke, in *Folklore of Canada*, says that these jokes are typical of the "fool Irishmen" stories that were common in North America in the 19th century, the height of Irish immigration. Later, many of same jokes targeted other immigrant groups, such as Ukrainians.

Pat and Mike, they were traveling along the road and they come to a farm house. So Mike says to Pat, "Pat, you'll have to make believe you're deef and dumb, so we can get somethin' to eat."

So they went to the door. Mike says, "Madam, will you please give my brother and me something to eat, he's deef and dumb."

The lady says, "Why sure. It's too bad your brother is deef and dumb."

Pat speaks up and says, "Bejabers, madam, it is that."

Jokes not only make us laugh—they also reveal something about our beliefs and traditions.

The ethnic joke may be inevitable in North America, given the rich diversity of immigrant populations that have been thrown into close proximity. Often one group feels the need to show its "superiority" by putting down another group, either on the basis of intelligence or appearance. Many people groups have been the butt of this type of humor, including the Irish, Scandinavians, Italians, and Jews. Ethnic jokes reveal North America's darker side. They demonstrate that humor is not always kind or constructive.

Martin Luther King, Jr. used the powerful traditions of African American preaching to bring change to our world.

SIX

Preaching and Praying
Spiritual Speech

Jonathan Edwards' powerful 18th-century sermon portrays an angry and frightening image of God.

S PEECH IS USED in names, in political persuasion, in advertising, in jokes made to help people cope with a difficult world, and to boast one's self image. But in the earliest years of the United States, preaching and praying were honored as the most important kind of speech.

Christianity was the foundation of Puritan life, an early American culture that has been called "christocentric" (centered around Jesus Christ). The preachers, as spokesmen of the Word of God, held a place of high esteem and honor among the people. As "shepherds," or leaders who cared for their congregations as a shepherd would care for his sheep, their words of instruction and admonition were heeded carefully.

One such preacher, Jonathan Edwards, delivered a sermon in 1735 that is still remembered today, called "Sinners in the Hands of an Angry God." Some of the most famous lines reflect his concern for the eternal destiny of his parishioners:

Sinner! Consider the fearful danger you are in: it is a great furnace of wrath, a wide and bottomless pit, full of the fire of wrath, that you are held over in the hand of that God, whose wrath is provoked and incensed as much against you, as against many of the damned in hell. You hang by slender thread, with the flames of divine wrath flashing about it, and ready every moment to singe it, and burn it asunder; and you have no interest in any Mediator, and nothing to lay hold of to save yourself, nothing to keep off the flames of wrath, nothing of your own, nothing that you

ever have done, nothing that you can do, to induce God to spare
you one moment. . . .

Edwards went on to explain that:

. . . now you have an extraordinary opportunity, a day wherein
Christ has thrown the door of mercy wide open, and stands call-
ing and crying with a loud voice to poor sinners . . . many that
were very lately in the same miserable condition that you are in
are now in a happy state, with their hearts filled with love to Him
who has loved them, and washed them from their sins in His own
blood, and rejoicing in hope of the glory of God. . . .

Edwards urged his listeners to ac-
cept what Christ had done for them in
dying on the cross, pleading with them
to "awake and fly from the wrath to
come." So powerful were his words that
great numbers of people experienced a
religious **revival** in the church there in
Northampton, Massachusetts. Some
consider this intense religious response
to Edwards' speaking to be an early part of or a precursor to an
even greater movement called the "Great Awakening," which
took place in New England from 1740 to 1743.

The Great Awakening affected 150 churches over an area including New England, New York, New Jersey, Pennsylvania,
Maryland, and Virginia. The preacher at the epicenter of this later
movement was George Whitefield, who came to New England in
1740. Whitefield's own account of his time in Boston, where so
many (eventually up to 15,000 people) crowded to hear him that
services had to be moved outside, says:

WESTERN FOLK NAMES FOR CLERGY AND CHURCH

church-agents
devil-dodgers
gospel-grinders
gospel-pounders

hymn-howlers
sky-pilots
gospel-mills
soul-grub (sermons)

O how the Word (meaning the Bible) did run. It rejoiced my heart to see such numbers greatly affected, so that some of them, I believe, could scarcely refrain from crying out, that the place was no other than a Bethel and the gate of heaven. Many wept exceedingly, and cried out under the Word, like persons that were hungering and thirsting after righteousness. The Spirit of the Lord was upon them all.

The results of Whitefield's powerful preaching were dramatic, as recorded by A. Skevington Wood in *The Inextinguishable Blaze: Spiritual Renewal and Advance in the 18th Century:*

No less than thirty religious societies were formed in the city. Churches were overcrowded. Ministers preached in private houses almost every evening. . . . It was said that the very face of Boston was strangely altered. Even the street loafers no longer made themselves objectionable and the taverns were well-nigh deserted.

Preaching continued to be highly regarded in the 1800s. White churches were not the only ones that influenced this aspect of folk culture. African American congregations developed their own style of church service, far more interactive than those held in Anglo churches. The African American preacher spoke a sentence or group of sentences, and those in the pews responded enthusiastically, so that the "sermon" seemed almost a joint effort. Fredericka Bremer, of Cincinnati, recorded such a service in 1850, and much of what she observed is still practiced today. Ac-

---

Throughout the history of North America, people have enjoyed poking fun at their "holy men," especially if they spy any inconsistency between their speech and their conduct. This story deals with the subject of lying:

Three chaplains in the armed forces were playing cards in their tent while they discussed the subject of honesty.

"Sometimes lying can't be avoided," said the Catholic priest.

"Sometimes it's necessary," agreed the Protestant minister.

"Never!" disagreed the rabbi. "One must *never* lie!"

Just then the commanding officer entered the tent and the chaplains tried frantically to hide their cards.

"Men," the officer asked, "were you playing cards, against all my orders?"

"Not me," said the priest.

"Nor I," answered the minister.

The officer turned to the rabbi. "And what about you, Chaplain Goldfarb? Were you playing cards?"

"If these two gentleman are not playing cards, with whom could I be playing?" asked the Rabbi.

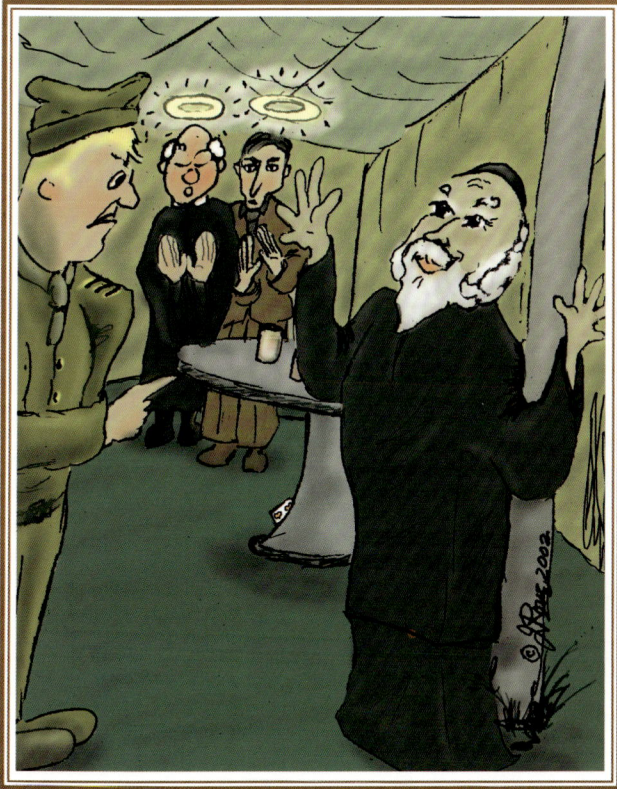

"With whom could I be playing?"

cording to her account (recorded in *A Treasury of African American Folklore* by Harold Courlander), the preacher began in this way:

> *"How shall we know that God is with us? Let us look at the question thus."*
> He then boldly sketched out a picture of an enslaved people as oppressed in every way, but not the less "increasing in numbers and im-

Religion and speech are connected.

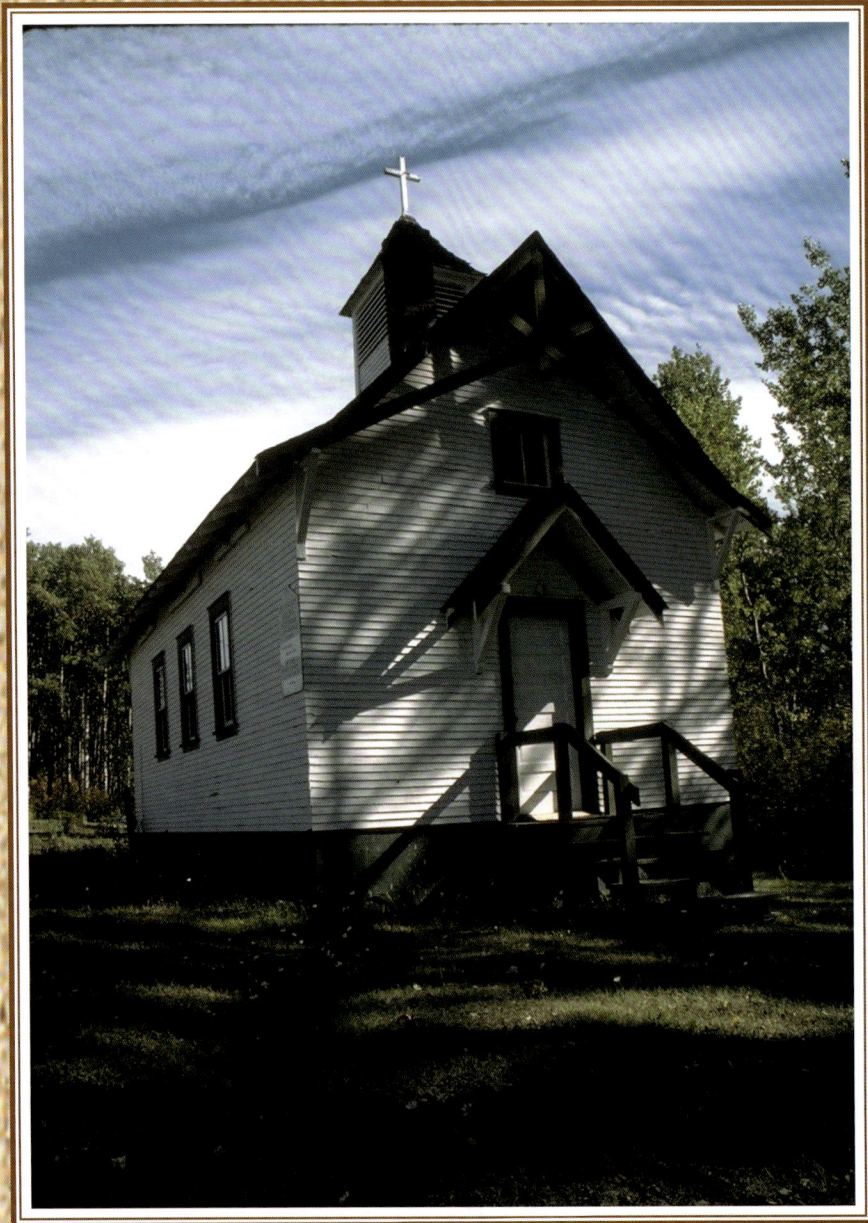

Small country churches were the scene of fiery preaching in the 18th and 19th centuries—and they still are today.

> The words that the mouth utters comes from the overflowing of the heart.
>
> —*Jesus Christ*

proving themselves, purchasing their own freedom from slavery (cries of "Yes! yes!" "Oh, glory!" throughout the church); purchasing land (shouts of joy); ever more and more land (increasing shouts); buying houses . . . and still larger houses (increasing jubilation and stamping of feet); building churches (still louder cries); still more and larger churches (louder and still louder cries, movement, stamping of feet and clapping of hands); . . . This, then, will show us, my brethren, that God is with us. Let us not forsake Him; for He will lead us out of captivity, and make of us a great people!" (extreme delight and joy, with the cry of "Amen!" "Yes, yes!" "Oh, glory!" and so on). The congregation was for several minutes like a stormy sea."

The tradition of African American preaching is still a powerful force in North America. Its strength and influence was made evident in 1960s in the sermons of Martin Luther King, Jr.; his passionate speech lit the fires against racism.

The words of the clergy, of all races and religions, remain one of the most powerful forces in shaping American culture today. Each religious tradition has its own style, found in the folk speech patterns of its people—but whatever the style, whatever the religion, speech and faith are still powerfully connected.

Whatever the regional dialect, speech has power.

SEVEN

Utterance and Meaning
Shaping the World with Speech

Speakers influence people's opinions, educate, and enlighten.

S TICKS AND STONES *may break my bones,*
But words will never hurt me.

Most children who know that couplet—and adults who remember it from their own childhood—realize just how false it is. It may be nearer the truth to say that almost nothing has as much power to hurt us as words do.

The power of words is expressed throughout history, in myths and ancient tales. There the idea is sometimes expressed as the immense power of a single word. Modern authors incorporate this idea in their writings, as C. S. Lewis did in the first of "The Chronicles of Narnia," *The Magician's Nephew.*

When Digory and Polly, the book's characters, find themselves in another world named Charn, they see that it lies in total ruin. They find themselves in front of the awesome and terrible queen Jadis; Jadis confesses that she herself is responsible for the ruin because she used the Deplorable Word. She then tells them the word's secret, explaining that it

> *. . . had long been known to the great kings of our race that there was a word which, if spoken with the proper ceremonies, would destroy all living things except the one who spoke it. But the ancient kings were weak and soft-hearted and bound themselves and all who should come after them with great oaths never even to seek after the knowledge of that word. But I learned it in a secret place and paid a terrible price to learn it.*

Like the Deplorable Word in this fictional account, words and speech have great power, both to destroy and to create. The Christian New Testament speaks of the "Word" as a term for God's communication to humanity through Christ. In the Book of Luke, we see the constructive power of speech, when Christ says:

> Let your conversation be always full of grace, seasoned with salt. . . .
>
> —*Colossians 4:15 (from the Christian New Testament)*

The spirit of the Lord is upon me because he has anointed me; he has sent me to announce good news to the poor, to proclaim release for prisoners and recovery of sight for the blind; to let the broken victims go free, to proclaim the year of the Lord's favor.

In a similar way, in the Old Testament Book of Genesis, God "speaks" the world into being.

The speech of ordinary people continues to have power in our world today. For instance, *Washington Post* journalist Dim Bivens noted that adolescent slang is helping to heal the terrible wounds left by the September 11, 2001 terrorist attacks on the United States. He writes:

It's just six months since Sept. 11, but that's enough time for the vocabulary of one of the country's most frightening days to become slang for teenagers of all backgrounds, comic relief in school hallways and hangouts.

> Let your conversation be without malice or envy, for it is a sign of tractable and commendable nature; and in all causes of passion admit reason to govern.
>
> —*from George Washington's Rules of Civility*

If you your lips would keep from
    slips,
Five things observe with care:
Of whom you speak, to whom you
    speak,
And how and when and where.

—*folk rhyme*

All meanings, ideas, intentions,
desires, emotions, items of knowledge
are embodied in speech, are rooted in
it and branch out of it.

—*Ancient Laws of Manu*

"It's like 'you're as blind as the FBI' is an insult," offered Morgan Hubbard, 17, a senior at Quince Orchard High School in Gaithersburg, Md., where students have picked up on the phrase from an Internet game.

"If you totally forgot about a test and didn't study, people might call you a 'CIA officer' or ask if you have 'any intelligence capabilities,'" said Najwa Awad, a Palestinian American student at J.E.B. Stuart High School in Falls Church, Va. "Sept. 11 has been such a stressful thing that it's OK to joke a little bit. . . ."

. . . Language has always been as malleable and erratic as the day's headlines, and young people have always been some of the most innovative and playful in linking world events to their daily vernacular. But it's more than what it seems on the surface. . . .

Only popular comics on television, radio and the Internet have as much influence on the national parlance as do brazen adolescents with their energy and uninhibited desire to craft their own language. . . .

Across North America, the speech of ordinary people varies from region to region—and yet speech is what also connects groups of people together. Through speech we communicate both our differences and our similarities; we express our longings, frustrations, and joys; we claim and shape the world around us, so that

Speech connects us—even across the miles.

we can interact with that world creatively and productively. Speech can have great destructive power—but its creative power is equally as great.

Across North America, each region has its own unique and powerful way of speaking. These words tell us something about the geography, the foods, and the ways of living in each area. Some words may enter into the mainstream of North American language, while others may be unique expressions of a particular way of life.

Here are some examples of Newfoundland words and their meanings:

angishore	a weak, miserable person
ballyrag	to abuse
bannikin	a small tin cup
barrisway	a lagoon at a river mouth
bedlamer	year-old seal
chucklehead	a stupid person
chinch	to stow tightly
clobber	an untidy state
come-from-away	tourist
doter	old seal
douse	to give a quick blow
drung	a narrow, rocky lane
drook	a valley with steep, wooded sides
duff	pudding of flour, fat pork, and molasses
dulse	a kind of seaweed
dudeen	a pipe
faddle	a bunch of firewood
floaters	fishermen on board schooners, who use cod traps
frappe	a rope with blocks to moor a boat
funk	bad-smelling air
gandy	pancake
gulvin	the stomach of a codfish
gowdy	awkward
huffed	vexed

jinker	one who brings bad luck
lashins	plenty
lolly	soft ice beginning to form in the harbor
lops	a sea with small waves
mauzy	misty
nish	tender, fragile
planchen	the floor
prog	food
puddock	stomach
rawny	thin, bony
scrawb	scratch with the nails
scut	a dirty mean person
sish	ice broken by the surf
slob	ice newly frozen
smidge	a stain
sloo	to get out of the way
slieveen	a liar
squabby	soft as jelly
switchel	cold tea
teeveen	patch on a boat
tole	entice with bait
tuckamore	low clump of trees
yarry	alert, wide awake
yaffle	an armful of dried fish

Further Reading

Courlander, Harold. *Afro-American Folklore.* New York: Marlowe, 1996.

Craughwell, Thomas J. *Alligators in the Sewers and 222 Other Urban Legends.* New York: Black Dog and Leventhal, 1999.

Cunningham, Keith, ed. *The Oral Tradition of the American West.* Little Rock, Ark.: August House, 1990.

Libal, Autumn. *Folk Proverbs and Riddles.* Philadelphia: Mason Crest, 2003.

Osborne, Mary Pope. *American Tall Tales.* New York: Alfred A. Knopf, 1991.

For More Information

American Folklore Society
afsnet.org

Folklore Society
www.folklore-society.com

Folk Speech
pinoystuff.com/folklore/folkspeech/folkspeech.htm

Folklore of Newfoundland
www.heritage.nf.ca

Regional Vocabulary
www.wordplay.com/tourism/folklore

Glossary

Euphemisms   Agreeable or inoffensive expressions or words substituted for ones that may offend or suggest something unpleasant.

Hyperbole   An extravagant exaggeration.

Indigenous   Having originated in and being produced in a particular region or environment.

Intensifiers   Words that intensify or strengthen speech.

Jargon   The technical and specialized vocabulary of a specific activity or group; its words are often abbreviated or simplified.

Linguistics   The study of human speech including the units, nature, structure, and modification of language.

Middle English   The English in use from the 12th to the 15th centuries.

Nomenclature   A system for providing names and designations.

Onomastics   The study of names.

Revival   A period of awakened religious fervor.

Slang   An informal, nonstandard form of language used by a particular group.

Striker   A blacksmith's helper who swings the sledgehammer.

Tinker   A traveling mender and seller of household goods.

Index